Discovering *ART*

Anime and Manga

John Allen

ReferencePoint
Press®

San Diego, CA

About the Author

John Allen is a writer who lives in Oklahoma City.

© 2015 ReferencePoint Press, Inc.
Printed in the United States

For more information, contact:
ReferencePoint Press, Inc.
PO Box 27779
San Diego, CA 92198
www.ReferencePointPress.com

LIBRARY OF CONGRESS CATALOGING-IN-PUBLICATION DATA

Allen, John, 1957–
  Anime and manga / by John Allen.
     pages cm. — (Discovering art)
  Includes bibliographical references and index.
  ISBN-13: 978-1-60152-696-0 (hardback)
  ISBN-10: 1-60152-696-2 (hardback)
  1. Comic books, strips, etc.—Japan—Juvenile literature. 2. Animated television programs—Japan—Juvenile literature. 3. Animated films—Japan—Juvenile literature. I. Title.
  NC1700.A45 2014
  741.5'952—dc23
                                                              2014011108

Contents

Anime and Manga

Among the films nominated for the 2014 Academy Awards were two animated films from Japan. One was Shuhei Morita's *Possessions*, nominated for Best Animated Short. The other was Hayao Miyazaki's feature-length film *The Wind Rises*. The Miyazaki film's nomination was interesting in several ways. For one thing, Miyazaki had already won an Oscar for Best Animated Feature in 2002 for his brilliant fantasy *Spirited Away*. And unlike the usual animated films featuring funny animals or based on fairy tales—such as fellow 2014 nominee *Frozen*, based on Hans Christian Andersen's "The Snow Queen"—*The Wind Rises* tells the very human story of a real-life Japanese engineer who dedicates his life to a dream. That dream is to design aircraft; specifically, fighter planes that his country will use to wage war. While many critics praised the film's beauty and grandeur, some expressed misgivings. They pointed out that while the film depicts the awfulness of warfare, it does not dwell on the atrocities committed by Japan's military before and during the Second World War. "The main worry is that people will make a judgment about the film before they see it," according to Fran Krause, a professor of character animation at California Institute of the Arts. "There is a lot of subtlety to Miyazaki's work, and this film in particular will require a lot of benefit of the doubt that people these days don't often have."[1] The controversy shows how Japanese film animation, called anime, has developed into a serious art form capable of delighting children with humor and beautiful imagery while igniting debate over its treatment of adult themes. This ability to appeal to all ages is shared by manga, the Japanese form of comics. Since their beginnings in the post–World War II period, anime and manga have developed a huge following not only in Japan but worldwide. They definitely are more than frivolous "cartoons" and "funny books" for kids.

Like other popular art forms, anime and manga have a sprawling, chaotic history with many "waves" and periods of change. Artists such as Osamu Tezuka, whose *Astro Boy* and *Kimba the White Lion* are only two of many classic creations, and the aforementioned Hayao Miyazaki pushed the boundaries of what Japanese animation could express. In the 1980s, considered by many a "golden age," a number of darker, more violent works appeared, such as the groundbreaking sci-fi movie *Akira*, which appealed to fans of alternative films and music. The 1990s brought female-oriented anime that was created by women, as well as the smash-hit adventures of Pokémon for kids. In the 2000s many American fans became hooked by watching some of the most radical anime on Adult Swim, the late-night programming block on the Cartoon Network. By that time it was commonplace to read critics' praise of anime as a serious, wide-ranging medium. As art forms, anime and manga have progressed from their simple cartoonish roots to become beautifully detailed visual art that can tell a variety of stories with imaginative force.

Words in Context
anime
Animation produced in Japan, whether drawn by hand or computer generated.

Anyone with an eye on pop culture today is familiar with the characteristic features of anime and manga: youths with large eyes, small mouths, and spiky or flowing hair; gigantic robots that shoot blasts of energy; impossibly agile ninja and samurai; and plump little creatures with adorable faces. Anime's characters are found in films, TV series, video games, and commercials. There are action figures, lunchboxes, greeting cards, and Halloween costumes based on anime and manga characters. Some anime and manga look back to Hollywood cartoons like *Mickey Mouse* and *Popeye*, while others share features with the superhero sagas of American comic books. Since the worldwide success of the *Astro Boy* TV series in the early 1960s—a character that originated in manga—anime has become a huge industry in Japan, with writers, artists, and animators working furiously in production lines to satisfy the demand for new films and series. As for manga, it is even more popular. Japanese of all ages regularly read manga in comic books or in collected book editions. There are lighthearted stories for small children, adventure stories for older children, edgy sci-fi tales for teenagers, historical and romantic fiction for adults, and even soap operas about workplace intrigue for those climbing the corporate ladder. Together, these art forms have created a look and a style of storytelling that has become popular beyond the shores of Japan and entertained millions of readers and viewers worldwide.

While a number of anime and manga draw inspiration from Western models, it is the uniquely Japanese elements that attract many fans. For example, unlike characters in most Western cartoons anime characters often display aspects of both good and evil, and plots rarely resolve into a traditional happy ending. Cultural details that Japanese audiences take for granted can seem mysterious and glamorous to viewers in other cultures. Stories refer to the Shinto religion, Buddhism, and Confucianism as a matter of course. Writers

Hayao Miyazaki's beautiful hand-drawn animation shines in a scene from his Academy Award–winning *Spirited Away*. Miyazaki's stories and art represent the height of anime.

and artists concentrate on expressing powerful emotions in new ways. A character may change shape or be drawn in a different style during a crisis. The setting itself is often used to stress a character's emotional state. Manga artists are also expert at using cinematic techniques to enhance the emotional impact of a scene. Odd details, such as a character's sudden bloody nose, can indicate feelings of love or lust to a Japanese audience. The Japanese fascination with robots and electronics has led to an entire genre called mecha, with robots that seek either to serve humankind or to conquer it. Several manga and anime works have dealt with the atomic bombs dropped on Hiroshima and Nagasaki and the aftermath of these events. Concern about the environment is another frequent theme. As seen in the Miyazaki controversy, the history of anime and manga is inseparable from Japan's postwar history, social and economic development, and relationship with the West. These art forms have arguably become Japan's most important cultural exports in the modern age.

Words in Context
manga
The Japanese form of comics, from a word that means "whimsical pictures."

Chapter One

Manga: Pioneers and Early Development

The building, with its silvery glass-domed tower, looks like a space-age lab on a comic book page. Located in a small town about 12.4 miles (20 km) northwest of Osaka, Japan, the Osamu Tezuka Manga Museum is dedicated to manga's most famous artist. Every month the museum attracts thousands of Tezuka's fans as well as fans of manga in general. Etched on the building's titanium walls are images of Tezuka's best-loved characters, including Astro Boy, Phoenix, Leo, and Princess Knight. The first floor takes visitors through the events of Tezuka's life, while the second floor presents exhibits on the best manga artists of the past and present. Children and adults alike enjoy browsing in the large library of manga and watching videos of Tezuka's anime features and experimental cartoons. The basement even contains a life-size talking puppet of Tezuka in his studio, explaining the details of his profession. The museum is a testament to Tezuka's role as a cultural hero in Japan and to the continuing popularity of manga as an art form.

The Roots of Manga

Though Tezuka is an honored father of manga, the art form's roots go back to the centuries-old love of expressive drawings among the

Japanese. The kanji characters of the Japanese language, adopted from Chinese ideograms, are themselves like simple drawings. Calligraphy, which is still practiced in Japan, combines drawing and writing. As early as the twelfth century, a priest named Toba Sojo made playful brushstroke drawings of monkeys, foxes, and rabbits to tell stories on a set of scrolls. In these "Animal Scrolls," the characters behave like humans. Like today's manga, the scrolls were read from right to left. In the early eighteenth century, cartoon books called *toba-e* (named after Toba Sojo) contained funny caricatures of long-legged little men committing the foibles of everyday life. The late eighteenth century brought *kibyoshi*, "yellow-cover" books that used simple drawings to tell topical stories or even to satirize those in authority.

Even more important as an influence on today's manga was the genre of wood-block prints called *ukiyo-e*—"pictures of the floating world." Beginning as crude black-and-white prints of scenes from Yoshiwara, the red-light district of what is now Tokyo, the ukiyo-e eventually improved in quality and began to address many different subjects, including fashion, interesting places and people, the stars of the popular Kabuki theater, and legends from history. These prints became widely popular among ordinary Japanese and were collected into books. Like many of today's manga, they were cheap, lively entertainment that took delight in everyday life. Some prints featured ghosts and *yokai*, or mythical Japanese monsters. The print artist Katsushika Hokusai, born in 1760, became a master of ukiyo-e, developing it into a sophisticated art form. Hokusai created series of beautiful woodblock prints such as *Thirty-Six Views of Mount Fuji*. Famous images like his *Great Wave Off Kanagawa*, created in the 1820s, influenced manga and anime artists like Hayao Miyazaki with their flowing lines and careful composition. It was Hokusai who also coined the term *manga*, which translates roughly to "whimsical drawings." His collection called *Hokusai Manga* features sketches of landscapes and details of

> **Words in Context**
> *ukiyo-e*
> Black-and-white or full-color woodblock prints that were very popular among ordinary Japanese in the nineteenth century and have been influential on manga and anime graphic styles.

The influence of Katsushika Hokusai's woodblock print series *Thirty-Six Views of Mount Fuji* can be seen in the work of contemporary anime and manga artists. Pictured is *In the Wall of the Great Wave,* one of the scenes from Hokusai's series.

nature as well as humorous drawings of people. Later in the century, old ukiyo-e prints turned up in Europe as packing paper in shipments of Japanese tea. Impressionist painters such as Edouard Manet, Vincent Van Gogh, Paul Gauguin, and Henri Toulouse-Lautrec fell in love with these beautiful images and adopted their use of intricate patterns and vivid colors.

Western influence reached Japan beginning in 1854, when Commodore Matthew Perry of the US Navy opened trade with the Japanese, ending the Edo period, a 250-year period of isolation. In the late 1800s Japanese cartoonists began to create satirical drawings with dialogue balloons like those in the British humor magazine *Punch.* Soon Japanese artists were risking punishment by lampooning those in authority. In 1905 Rakuten Kitazawa started the wildly successful *Tokyo Puck,* the first manga magazine with stories and regular characters. Kitazawa and Ippei Okamoto, another popular artist, traveled abroad and learned about cartoonists in other countries, including the United States. Both men admired American comic strips like *Bringing Up Father* and used them as models for their own work. By the 1920s and 1930s, there were large monthly magazines for manga such as *Shonen Club* (Boys' Club) and *Shojo Club* (Girls' Club). These magazines, with their lighthearted

The Look of Manga Characters

New readers of manga are struck by the typical look of the characters. Most have very large eyes and tiny mouths. As with many features of manga, this look originated with Osamu Tezuka. Tezuka was inspired by the drawing styles of American animators such as Walt Disney and Max Fleischer. Disney's Mickey Mouse was drawn with large cartoonish eyes, while Fleischer's Betty Boop, based on the flappers of the 1920s, had enormous round eyes with spiky eyelashes and a tiny pouting mouth. Tezuka adapted this look for characters such as Astro Boy. Tezuka's popularity and mentor status among early manga artists help explain why the big-eyed look caught on. Large eyes also make the characters look cuter or more appealing. Younger characters usually have the largest eyes, while older ones may be drawn more realistically. Another factor in how the characters look is the Japanese love of strong emotions. "Absolutely everything in Manga is made to feel like it's bursting forth from the page," according to manga artists Ilya-San and Yahya El-Droubie. "Japanese readers respond to big faces, bigger expressions, and larger-than-life emotions. Even subtle moods that are not so easily defined are expressed to the core." As the eyes are considered the windows of the soul, manga artists tend to exaggerate their size to make them more expressive.

Ilya-San and Yahya El-Droubie, *How to Draw Manga-Style*. New York: Chartwell, 2010, p. 24.

tone, show a strong Western influence. Comic strips like *Norakuro* (*Black Stray*), about a heroic puppy that joins the Imperial army, reflect Japan's turn towards militarism in the 1930s. *Norakuro* sold a million copies when compiled into hardback books. World War II saw manga artists join the Japanese war effort by producing stories of battlefield courage and propaganda about the enemy. The most popular newspaper comic strip of the time, *Fuku-chan* (*Little Fuku*), underwent a name change to the more combative *Advance, Little Fuku!* Enemy leaders such as American president Franklin D. Roosevelt were drawn with fangs and claws. Even family-oriented manga depicted the difficulties of life during wartime.

Tezuka and a New Kind of Manga

Japan's surrender in 1945 ushered in a postwar period of shortages and economic hardship. War-weary citizens wanted to focus on rebuilding their lives and their society. They also wanted simple entertainment. Many newspaper comic strips presented humorous family situations about adjusting to lean times. One of the most popular strips was similar to the American comic strip *Blondie*. Hasegawa Machiko's *Sazae-san* features a wife who was an early example of the "liberated woman." Sazae runs the household and bosses her husband around to the disapproval of her tradition-minded neighbors. Machiko's comic strip proved so popular that it lasted until 1974, spinning off songs, a radio program, a TV series, and a live-action film. Besides reading comic strips, Japanese children and their parents also flocked to public parks to see *kamishibai*, or "paper theater." In these productions, traveling storytellers would present a sequence of hand-painted cardboard panels to tell a variety of exciting, eerie, or humorous tales. The artists would vary their voices, provide narration, and even offer sound effects. At its height, there were more than ten thousand *kamishibai* artists performing in Japan. Several prominent manga artists got their start drawing and presenting *kamishibai*, earning money by selling sweets to their audience.

In the lean years after the war, people had little money to spend on manga. As a result, artists concentrated their production into two main areas. One was manga in the form of magazines that were bor-

Children gather around a storyteller in a Tokyo park for a traditional *kamishibai,* or "paper theater," performance in the 1990s. Some prominent manga artists began their careers in this way.

rowed from rental libraries for small fees. Another was manga called *akabon,* or "red books." *Akabon* were pocket-size comics printed in black and white on cheap paper with garish red covers. They were sold on city streets by vendors. Artists were paid next to nothing for these two-hundred-page editions, but they also enjoyed tremendous freedom to create their own stories.

One artist who took advantage of the popularity of *akabon* was Tezuka. A twenty-year-old medical student in Osaka, the center of *akabon* production, Tezuka brought an intellectual approach to creating comics. His parents had instilled in him a love of the arts, and he had been drawing his own comic strips since childhood. His first big success in manga was a two-hundred-page epic called *Shin-takarajima* (*New Treasure Island*). It is an update of Robert Louis

Stevenson's novel *Treasure Island* that Tezuka developed with the artist Sakai Shichima. Tezuka's main influence, however, was not literature or other manga but film. He loved foreign movies and the cartoons of Walt Disney and realized that certain film methods could be adapted to manga. "I began to introduce cinematic techniques into my composition," Tezuka writes in his autobiography. "The models for this were the German and French movies I saw in my days as a student. I manipulated close-ups and angles, of course, and tried using many panels or even many pages in order to capture faithfully movements and facial expressions that once would have been taken care of with a single panel."[2] In *New Treasure Island* Tezuka tried different points of view, page layouts, and panel sizes. Even the sound effects were written in bold characters. Young readers almost felt like they were watching a new kind of adventure movie. Other manga artists were amazed and inspired. Years later the manga artist duo known as Fujiko Fujio published a comic about their excitement upon first reading Tezuka's manga debut. With no prior publicity, *Shintakarajima* sold hundreds of thousands of copies.

> **Words in Context**
> *cinematic techniques*
> Camera effects used in movies and adapted to manga, such as close-ups, zooms (or progressively closer shots), odd angles, and panoramic views.

Manga Production Expands

Tezuka's success led to a huge demand for manga in the early 1950s. Publishers in Tokyo jumped into the comics business, and the city became the new center of manga production. After many visits, Tezuka finally moved there in 1954, joining a flood of artists hoping to take advantage of the manga phenomenon. "At that time, comics artists in Japan were not highly regarded," according to Helen McCarthy, author of several books on Japanese manga. "They worked punishing schedules for low rates of pay, with no job security and very little respect from the majority of people."[3] However, the example that Tezuka had set convinced many artists that manga was an accessible medium for new talent and did not require any special education or

Tokiwa-so, the Legendary Manga Apartment Building

With the success of Osamu Tezuka and the boom in manga in the 1950s, young artists flocked to Tokyo, the center of manga publishing. They hoped to get jobs drawing for the best magazines, such as *Manga Shonen*. With little money, they searched for the cheapest lodgings available. One popular place was Tokiwa-so, a run-down two-story apartment building built before World War II. Tezuka himself occupied room 14—reason enough for aspiring manga artists to rent their own rooms there. The ramshackle building had no bathtubs and only cold water trickling out of the taps. Most of the struggling youths could barely make their rent payments each month. Yet they all dreamed of becoming successful *mangaka*, or manga artists, like their hero.

Two of the residents were Hiroshi Fujimoto and Motoo Abiko. This artistic duo, working under the pen name Fujiko Fujio, would become famous for creating *Doraemon*, one of the world's best-selling manga. The pair learned about a vacancy at Tokiwa-so from Tezuka himself, who was moving to another building. The great artist even helped them with the deposit. "Those days had a big influence on me," says Abiko in an interview. "In those days, being a mangaka was an unrealistic job. Mr. Tezuka was the shining star for us. . . . I was encouraged by all the struggling friends around me." Among those struggling friends were artists such as Shotaro Ishinomori and Fujio Akatsuka, who would go on to become legendary in the field of manga.

ComiPress, "Fujiko Fujio (A) Talks About Life at Tokiwa-so," January 19, 2008. www
.comipress.com.

training. In fact, the popular magazine *Manga Shonen* accepted manga submissions from readers and published the best of them. Contributors to *Manga Shonen* in the early 1950s included teenage artists who would dominate the manga industry for a generation, while others went on to become actors, novelists, designers, and screenplay writers.

While the artists who drew manga series for the Tokyo magazines were considered the industry's elite, other artists were also experimenting with story comics. In Osaka a group created hardcover comics aimed at the professional lending libraries for much less pay than offered in Tokyo. Some magazines, such as *Kage* (*Shadow*) and *Machi* (*City*), were designed exclusively for the lending libraries, with their older readership of high school students and factory workers. Like Tezuka, the Osaka artists employed cinematic ideas and complex plots in their manga. However, instead of using Tezuka's style of simple rounded characters based on Disney's animation, they drew in a more realistic manner in order to present adult-oriented plots and themes. The new genre came to be known as *gekiga*, or "dramatic pictures." Both styles continue to be used in today's manga.

> **Words in Context**
> *gekiga*
> Literally, "dramatic pictures," a form of manga with plots and artwork geared to a more mature audience.

The Process of Creating Manga

In whatever style they employ, manga artists have to be creative and willing to work hard. Each installment of a popular series has to be completed on a tight deadline. *Mangaka*, or artists who produce manga, may work in an office or at home. One person may create both plot and artwork, or the artist may collaborate with others. However, the most popular manga are usually associated with a single creator, as with Tezuka's classics.

The artist begins with a story idea that will fill the required number of pages in an issue—often about twenty pages for each installment. Then he or she begins to lay out the pages, using a ruler to create the panel boxes. The first sketches may be done in blue pencil, which does not show up in reproduction. The main drawing is done with a graphite pencil—with a trusty eraser handy—and detail is added until each panel is complete. Once the artist is satisfied with a page of panels, including both layout and drawing, he or she (or another artist) then begins going over the pencil lines in black ink for the final artwork. Artists often use a variety of ink pens, from thick- to fine-point. Since manga is generally printed in black and white on flimsy paper, the artist may use areas of solid black sparingly to avoid problems of ink bleeding through. For shading, the artist uses cross-hatching, stippling, or prepared effects on transfer sheets. Manga, like comic books in the United States, have developed their own language of visual effects. For example, thin lines radiating outward can represent a shattering blow, a surge of energy, or radiant light. Parallel lines can show the speed of a pitched ball or a hurtling automobile. A character's arms or legs may be blurred to indicate fast movement. Manga artists strive to create dramatic poses for their characters with foreshortening of limbs and dramatic lighting effects. The artist also fills in dialogue balloons and adds sound effects—often with a tumble of large ideograms. Unlike Western comics, manga rarely feature boxes with scene-setting information, relying instead on detailed backgrounds and clear plot lines to keep the reader informed.

The process of creating manga is similar to that used for Western comics. However, manga has several unique features. For instance, manga magazines are read in the opposite way from Western comic books. What is the back cover of a Western comic is the front cover of a manga. Also, a page of manga reads from right to left, with the first panel on a page being the one in the upper right corner. When manga are translated for the American market, the order of the panels is generally rearranged—although as non-Japanese fans have become more sophisticated some of the best manga have been published in their Japanese format outside Japan. Manga also tend to have hundreds of pages and look like small phone books. Original manga in Japan are read and tossed aside. "When I first started to live in Japan," writes Danny Choo, a computer engineer and manga enthusiast, "I would see [the manga] that meant so much to me back in the UK just dumped out with the recyclable materials. At first I was surprised but then got used to it after understanding just how

How To Read Manga

In English, people read from left to right. In traditional Japanese manga, the action and dialogue move from right to left. This manga illustration shows the correct way to read the panels and word bubbles, beginning in the upper right-hand corner with 1A.

Word bubble order   Panel order

much Manga is a part of the lives of Japanese folks."[4] The most popular stories are reprinted in collectors' editions called *tankobon* with better quality paper.

Tezuka's Triumphant Career

Tezuka wasted no time in building on the popularity of his first manga. For the new Tokyo-based boys' magazines, he created two classic series, *Jungle Taitei* (*Jungle Emperor*) and *Tetsuwan Atomu* (*Astro Boy*). *Jungle Emperor* presents the adventures of a white lion that was raised by humans and upon returning to the jungle strives to control his aggressive nature. *Astro Boy* tells the Pinocchio-like story of a robot boy created and abandoned by one scientist only to be adopted by another. The little robot uses his rocketing speed and strength to fight for peace and justice—a theme that resonated with postwar Japanese readers. These pioneering works, however, are only a part of Tezuka's influential output. As the manga expert Frederik L. Schodt writes:

> **Words in Context**
> *stippling*
> Creating shading effects with small dots.

> Tezuka is an example of how one talented individual, born at the right time, can profoundly change the field he decides to work in. His heart was not in medicine, and when he eventually abandoned his scalpel to become a professional artist he brought to the medium of children's comics the cultivated mind of an intellectual, a fertile imagination, and the desire to experiment. Comics were merely a forum for Tezuka to express himself.[5]

Tezuka's tireless creativity led to classic series for all ages. In *Ribon no Kishi* (*Princess Knight*) he produced one of the first manga for girls. In *Black Jack* he drew upon his medical background for the adventures of an outlaw doctor. Through the years Tezuka increasingly explored adult themes and philosophical ideas in his manga. For example, the nine volumes of the series *Hi no Tori* (*Phoenix*) tell the story of humankind's quest for immortality and feature episodes set centuries ago in feudal Japan and thousands of years in the future. Besides his work in manga, Tezuka also adapted many of his stories for anime. When he died in 1989 at age sixty, he had created more than 150,000 pages of manga for hundreds of series. It was said that many Japanese mourned Tezuka's passing more than that of Emperor Hirohito, who had died one month before. Tezuka's legacy in Japan as the God of Manga is secure.

Chapter Two

Manga Becomes a Mature Art Form

Japanese both young and old are experienced consumers of manga. Comic magazines can be found everywhere in Japan, from barbershops and beauty salons to offices and factories. Manga fills the shelves at bookstores and secondhand shops and is also found in vending machines and special manga cafes. Kiosks at train stations do a brisk business at rush hour. A Tokyo office worker commuting on a train might pick up a two-inch thick manga magazine in one station, read it from cover to cover in a few minutes, and discard it at his final stop for someone else to enjoy. "In order to digest such a mass of comics, the Japanese have to be fast readers," writes Frederik L. Schodt. "According to an editor of Kodansha's *Shonen Magazine*, who must know about such things, on the average it takes the reader twenty minutes to finish a 320-page comic magazine. A quick calculation yields a breakdown of 16 pages a minute, or 3.75 seconds spent on each page."[6] One reason for this speedy consumption is the Japanese reader's familiarity with all the conventions of manga. Another is the manga artist's use of a purely visual language to tell stories. A battle between two samurai or robots may be presented in a wordless rush of images over several pages. In addition, manga artists have more pages to work with than their Western counterparts. When compiled into volumes, a single narrative can extend over two thousand pages. Filling the pages of popular manga on a tight schedule keeps artists hard at work at their drawing boards for long hours each week.

The Manga Boom

The workload for manga artists suddenly increased in the late 1950s when magazines went from a monthly to a weekly format. The change was due to the exploding popularity of manga—from Osamu Tezuka's imaginative series to the variety of new work created by *mangaka* who were inspired by his example. In postwar Japan, with television yet to become a widespread medium, young people sought cheap forms of entertainment. Publishers saw that the more manga they included in magazines for children, the better they sold. At the same time, older readers such as students and laborers who had grown up reading manga formed a ready market for the more sophisticated *gekiga* available through the rental libraries. With the new weeklies, manga artists who had hustled to meet monthly deadlines suddenly had four times more pages to fill. The result was new opportunities for young artists with ideas and a willingness to work.

> **Words in Context**
> *mangaka*
> Artists who create manga.

To deal with the new demand, artists like Tezuka began a production system that allowed them to output material more rapidly. A team of assistants was given specific tasks to complete. Young artists followed the main artist's instructions as to character development and story lines. Then they made drawings, inked drawings, or lettered the dialogue balloons and sound effects. This system, which is still in use today, allowed creators like Tezuka to produce several series at once.

By 1960 Japan's economy was beginning a rapid expansion. Ninety percent of Japanese households owned television sets. Young people with money to spend were buying more manga. Kodansha, one of Japan's largest book publishers, started *Shonen Magazine*, the first weekly devoted entirely to manga. Soon there were five weeklies for boys' comics and two for girls'. Helping to fuel the boom in manga were innovations in the technology of commercial presses, allowing for high volume print runs at low cost. By 1966 *Shonen Magazine* had a circulation of over 1 million. Twelve years later its competitor *Shonen Jump* was selling 5 million copies a week, making it Japan's best-selling magazine of any kind.

With young readers more willing to buy comics, the rental libraries disappeared, and the artists who had fed that market moved to Tokyo, the center of manga production. The comics medium was a wide-open field where imaginative artists could make a name for themselves quickly. Many of them turned away from the cartoonish style Tezuka used for his comics in order to present darker, more

Manga went through a boom in the late 1950s, thanks in large part to the popularity of the many imaginative series created by the renowned manga artist Osamu Tezuka (pictured). To meet demand, Tezuka and other artists created a new system for producing their art.

realistic stories suitable for adults. Tezuka's innovations, such as cinema-style montage and complex plotting, inspired artists such as Takao Saito, Sanpei Shirato, and Yoshihiro Tatsumi to experiment even further with their *gekiga* productions. Saito's *Golgo 13*, for example, presents the adventures of a mysterious professional assassin—a sort of Japanese James Bond. Begun in 1968, *Golgo 13* continues today as the longest-running manga series ever. Shirato created blood-soaked ninja sagas like *Kamui Den* (*Legend of Kamui*) for his own avant-garde monthly magazine. (A ninja was a secret mercenary fighter in feudal Japan.) Tatsumi, credited with inventing the term *gekiga* or "drama pictures," presented dark stories about jealousy and murder in a style that influenced many of his fellow artists. The success of these and other adult-oriented manga led Tezuka to create his own *gekiga*, including the epic series *Phoenix*.

Manga's Major Categories

Manga's success with readers both young and old led to the creation of several categories of manga. These groupings are based on the age and gender of the readers at which they are aimed. It is often difficult to isolate genres of manga since so many artists combine adventure, drama, mystery, comedy, and romance in their works. The major categories include the following:

Shonen manga is manga for boys. (The word *shonen* means "boy.") Its stories appeal to an adolescent male audience by focusing on young heroes who must overcome obstacles to reach a specific goal. The protagonists usually are psychologically generic so that the average reader can identify with them easily. The action-packed narratives are filled with colorful characters and dramatic set pieces. A good example of shonen manga is Akira Toriyama's long-running blockbuster series *Dragon Ball*, which debuted in *Shonen Jump* in 1984. Its protagonist, an alien boy named Goku, meets wondrous characters and trains in the martial arts on his quest for the magical dragon balls—lost balls that if collected will grant the possessor a single great wish. Another enormously popular shonen manga was Takehiko Inoue's *Slam Dunk*, a sports-

One well-known shonen manga, *Dragon Ball*, debuted in *Shonen Jump* in 1984. A later, English-language edition of the publication appears here. Shonen manga is aimed at adolescent boys and usually features stories about young heroes who must overcome obstacles.

themed comic about a delinquent gang leader who becomes a basketball star.

Many popular shonen manga series include robots and futuristic worlds. In fact, the Japanese fascination with giant robots led to

Invasion of the Giant Robots

Along with large-eyed heroines and quirky hairstyles, one of the most eye-catching aspects of manga is the giant robot. Young readers worldwide have thrilled to the spectacle of gigantic humanoid machines striding into battle with laser beams flashing. Many elements of mecha, the Japanese comics genre devoted to giant robots, can be traced back to Go Nagai's *Mazinger Z* series. Mazinger Z is a giant robot forged from Super Alloy Z and piloted by a daring, hotheaded sixteen-year-old hero named Kouji Kabuto. Kouji's grandfather developed the alloy from Japanium, a rare element found only at the base of Mt. Fuji. Kouji's weekly adventures saw him at the controls of Mazinger Z battling a variety of ancient mechanical beasts revived by the evil Dr. Hell.

From the series' start, manga fans loved the notion of piloting a huge robot. Nagai got the idea from watching frustrated drivers stuck in a traffic jam. He imagined an automobile that could sprout arms and legs and simply step over the other cars. "What I had in common with the children that were seeing robots was that I wanted to have this incredible power," Nagai told an interviewer. "I didn't equate giant robots with weapons, I wanted to give a teenaged character a suit of armor that would turn him into a hero." Nagai's creation has influenced all the later mecha classics, including the grittier robot sagas *Mobile Suit Gundam* and *Neon Genesis Evangelion*.

Quoted in Jeff Blagdon, "Rise of the Giant Robots: How One Japanese Cartoon Spawned a Genre." *The Verge*, December 13, 2012. www.theverge.com.

a whole genre of manga called mecha (derived from the Japanese abbreviation for the English word "mechanical"). The first mecha series was Go Nagai's *Mazinger Z*, which began in *Shonen Jump* in 1972. Tales of samurai (feudal Japanese warriors who lived by an elaborate code of honor) and stories of the Japanese criminal underworld are other popular subjects for shonen manga.

Shojo manga is manga for females. (While *shojo* means "girl," shojo manga may be written for young girls or for women.) Shojo manga was originally created by male artists and was similar to Western-style romance comics. The first weekly manga for girls was *Shojo Friend*, which began publishing in 1963. In the 1970s a flood of new female artists began to create shojo manga that experimented with new themes and styles of artwork and appealed more directly to the concerns of adolescent girls. "Today's shojo manga is an extensive genre with many different subgenres," writes Jacqueline Danziger-Russell, who studies female-oriented comics, "yet they are united by core themes, style, and aesthetic values. No matter whether the plots are fantastic or realistic, if they are more action-oriented or are emotionally based, there is typically a focus on relationships, romance, and personal development in shojo manga."[7] Thus while boys' comics in Japan usually unfold at rollicking speed, most shojo manga moves at a slower pace and tends to explore the feelings of its protagonists in greater detail. Illustrations for female-oriented comics concentrate on flowing designs of flowers, leaves, and clouds. In fact, one popular shojo magazine is entitled *Flowers and Dreams*. Shojo artists depict current fashions and hairstyles meticulously. Characters are drawn in a more exaggerated style; the huge, orblike eyes of the heroines are often highlighted with stars to emphasize a dreamy yearning. Typical of this style was Kimiko Uehara's *Maiko no Uta* (*Song of a Dancer*), set in the world of ballet. However, some Japanese female readers prefer action-packed adventure stories that are more like manga for boys. Tezuka introduced adventure stories for girls in the 1950s with *Ribon no Kishi* (*Princess Knight*), about a princess who is raised as a boy and vanquishes foes with her sword. *Princess Knight* influenced later manga classics for females such as Ryoko Ikeda's *Rose of Versailles*, which debuted in 1973. Its heroine is also raised as a male to succeed her father as leader of the royal guard before the French Revolution.

> **Words in Context**
> *mecha*
> Short for "mechanical," a manga genre that focuses on gigantic robots and complex technology.

Josei manga is manga produced for women. In the mid-1970s, female comics artists such as Miyako Maki and Masako Watanabe began to produce more sophisticated *gekiga*-style manga for an older female readership, from office workers to housewives. "These manga depicted the realities and obstacles of life after marriage, unlike shojo manga, which concentrated on finding true love," writes Mosami Toku, associate professor of art education at California State University. "For example, as her interests have matured and changed with age, Maki, who started as a girls' *mangaka* with sweet stories for young girls in the 1950s, has targeted the older audience of ladies' manga, creating artwork that is more personally relevant and interesting to her."[8] Maki also created her own versions of classic literature, such as *Tales of Genji*, which is based on the eleventh-century novel about the romantic life and aristocratic ambitions of the son of a Japanese emperor who is removed from the line of succession to the throne.

Kodomo manga, or manga for children, generally has simple, moralistic stories that teach young people how to behave with honesty, consideration, perseverance, and courage. These stories, which are usually stand-alone episodes rather than multipart sagas, feature cute human or animal characters. The Japanese slang word *chibi*, for "short person" or "small child," is often used to describe the drawing style for characters in kodomo manga.

One of the most famous kodomo series is *Doraemon*, created by the artist team Fujiko Fujio in 1969. In the series a boy named Nobita suffers failures at school and in everyday life until a blue robotic cat named Doraemon arrives from the future to help. Doraemon inevitably provides a futuristic gadget—plucked from his fourth-dimensional pocket—that saves the day by enabling Nobita to fix a problem or triumph over a bullying classmate. Doraemon is drawn in a round, cartoonish style that appeals to young readers. The series is filled with comic touches. For example, Doraemon has no ears, a robotic mouse having chewed them off and left him with a phobia about mice. Characters from the series are often referred to in Japanese culture, and Doraemon merchandise is a consistent seller.

Seinen manga, or manga for young men, draws upon the *gekiga* approach of more sophisticated stories and themes. Its popularity

One of the most famous manga series for children, *Doraemon*, is drawn in a round, cartoonish style that appeals to young readers. A scene from the series is pictured.

owes much to the generation that grew up reading manga. As cultural critic Matt Thorn points out:

> A boy born in 1950 would have been about nine years old when the medium of manga was revolutionized by the weekly format. He would have been in high school when the exciting developments of the mid to late sixties took place. He would have

been a college student (or worker) when the seinen genre had been firmly established. Another Japanese man born a year or two earlier would have already set manga aside by the time the weekly format was beginning to realize its potential, but the younger reader, never allowed a dull moment, would be hooked for life, as would every subsequent generation of Japanese.[9]

One of the best examples of seinen's possibilities is the breakthrough science-fiction series *Akira* by Katsuhiro Otomo. This dark, violent saga is considered by many to be one of manga's supreme masterworks. Set in 2030 in a neo-Tokyo built on the ashes from a blast that triggered World War III, *Akira* focuses on streetwise teenage friends Tetsuo and Kaneda. When Tetsuo begins to display psychic abilities, he is pursued by a government agency connected to a mysterious all-powerful figure known only as Akira. The series draws upon conventions of cyberpunk, a science-fiction subgenre that features advanced technology against a background of urban streets and societal breakdown. *Ghost in the Shell*, another landmark series, also makes use of ideas from cyberpunk as it tells the story of a specialized police unit that tracks cybercriminals. The success of these series has led to the creation of imaginative seinen manga in a wide array of genres, from martial arts and ninja tales to stories of the occult. Seinen manga also includes explicitly erotic material of every conceivable variety. Such artwork is common in Japanese culture, going back to the shunga woodblock prints that were popular in the nineteenth century. Western readers are often startled by the amount of sex and violence that appears in almost every category of manga and is accepted with a shrug by Japanese fans.

Innovations in Manga's Graphic Style

With Tezuka's cinema-inspired graphics a lesson well learned, manga artists have continued to experiment with how their stories are presented on the page. Today's manga often feature pages broken up into jagged panels like a broken pane of glass. Like a movie director blocking out a scene, manga artists lay out each page to emphasize a certain action or emotion. They make sure that the reader's eye will flow easily from panel to panel in a logical progression. They adjust the size and number of panels to control the flow of time in their stories. Fewer panels quicken the pace, while more panels slow the action. A single battle may spread out over dozens of pages with very little dialogue. One famous wordless confrontation between samurai unfolded for a tense series of panels as the glint of the rising sun ascended to the tips of their raised swords.

Manga artists strive to create the most dramatic effects possible. A character may burst outside the confines of the panels or come progressively closer in a series of zoom shots. Tiny panels can focus on details such as a ticking clock, trembling fingers, or a sweaty brow. Artists employ dramatic lighting and shadows to add to the emotional atmosphere. They vary the point of view to increase tension or provide emotional distance. Some artists enjoy playing with the form, as when a baseball pitcher's throwing motion is presented as an overlapping flow of drawings or a knife's blade slices through the page. Manga artists also make clever uses of bold *kanji* and *katakana*—different forms of script—for sound effects, and have developed a whole language of special words to represent sounds. Besides the usual words for explosions and fist-on-jaw impact, Japanese artists have developed sounds for almost everything that can be depicted. According to Schodt, "They have sounds that represent noodles being slurped (SURU SURU), umpteen types of rain (ZA, BOTSUN BOTSUN, PARA PARA), and the sudden flame from a propane cigarette lighter (SHUBO)."[10] Like the Zen *koan* (or paradox) about the sound of one hand clapping, artists also present the sound of no sound at all: an extended SHIIIIN.

If anything, female artists have been even more innovative in their graphic approach. A page of a typical shojo manga contains beautiful designs and patterns of flowers, vines, fabrics, feathers, and stars. The heroine's hair may curl around the dialogue balloons in elegant tendrils or frame the page in flowing tresses. A character's memories may be presented completely in a tumble of pictures.

Hiromu Arakawa and *Fullmetal Alchemist*

Drawing upon aspects of ancient alchemy and modern economics, Hiromu Arakawa's *Fullmetal Alchemist* shows the range of reference available to an imaginative manga artist. Born in 1973 and raised on a dairy farm in Hokkaido, Japan, Arakawa dreamed of becoming a *mangaka*. After high school she took oil painting classes while working on the family farm. She began her career in manga as an assistant to the artist Hiroyuki Eto. Eventually she got the opportunity to create her own manga. She had been reading about historical alchemists and their search for a philosopher's stone that would transmute any substance into gold. Her experiences on the family farm had also spurred an interest in economics. She combined these ideas in a magical storyline set in a world much like Europe during the Industrial Revolution. In Arakawa's tale, the philosopher's stone can create or alter human beings and is desperately sought by all sorts of characters. Arakawa also focuses on social issues and caring for orphans and refugees. The full saga, which ended in 2010, took up twenty-seven volumes. "When we finished the manga," Arakawa told a French interviewer, "I was surprised because I had been drawing this story for nine years and I was convinced that in the end, I would be sad, as in a breakup. When I submitted the last chapter, I was actually relieved. Not because I was glad it was over, but because I had the conviction I had told everything I wanted to."

Hiromu Arakawa, interview by *Animeland*, "Hiromu Arakawa Interview," Last Known Surroundings, *Animeland*, March 9, 2013. http://clewilan.tumblr.com.

Technology has also brought changes to the process of creating manga. Today's manga artists sometimes employ special software that assists them in laying out pages and adjusting lighting effects. It also can provide sophisticated airbrush effects that create a dreamy atmosphere or a sense of photorealism.

Manga Today

Technology may have dampened some of manga's popularity in Japan in the last decade. Many young people who once would have spent most of their spare time reading manga now spend it consulting their cell phones or communicating on social media. Manga magazines that reached peak sales of six million copies in 2000 now typically sell half that number. To counter the trend, publishers are experimenting with *keitai* manga, or manga created specifically for download to cell phones, with results that are promising but inconclusive. Streaming technology also enables manga fans to focus more on anime in order to follow the adventures of their favorite characters.

While demand for original manga has dropped off some, manga classics compiled in *tankobon* editions continue to rack up sales. Hiromu Arakawa's *Fullmetal Alchemist* and Naoki Urasawa's *Monster* are just two recent series that remain popular.

> **Words in Context**
> *airbrush*
> A small graphic tool that sprays ink or paint with compressed air to create effects of softness or seamless blending.

Manga also is influential in other areas of Japanese society and culture. Manga techniques are used in advertisements, textbooks, and instruction manuals. Contemporary artists such as Takashi Murakami create paintings based on manga-style illustrations, a postmodern art movement known as superflat. These "borrowings" suggest that manga will continue to have an impact on Japanese culture even if its golden age in print might have passed.

Chapter Three

The Early Years of Anime

At any San Diego ComicCon convention, where fans of comics and animation gather, a certain number of middle-aged baby boomers or younger enthusiasts will be dressed as race car drivers, each with a white helmet, a stuffed chimp on his or her shoulder, and maybe a steering wheel in hand. These are fans of *Speed Racer*, the animated series from Japan that began broadcasting in the United States in 1967. They know that the Japanese title of the series translates as *Mach GoGoGo!* and contains a triple pun that has to do with the hero's Japanese name (Gō Mifune), the name of his sportscar (the Mach 5 or *Mach-gō*, in Japanese), and the English word "go." They can briskly identify the Americanized main characters, including the young driver, Speed; Speed's girlfriend, Trixie; his trusty mechanic, Sparky; and his pet monkey, Chim Chim. They love to repeat the famous tagline *Go Speed Racer, Go!* And they might share a chuckle about the clumsiness of the animation—particularly the characters' limited movement and rapid-fire dubbed dialogue. "This show is remembered for its goofy character designs, [primitive] animation and atrocious dub, as well as its memorable characters and over-the-top sensibilities,"[11] remarks the website TV Tropes. *Speed Racer* was many Americans' first encounter with anime, the Japanese form of animation. Anime would go on to achieve huge worldwide success with a variety of imaginative series and remains today one of Japan's chief cultural exports.

Anime's Beginnings

Few examples of Japanese animation from the early twentieth century exist today. This is due not only to losses over time but also to the 1923 Great Kanto earthquake that leveled much of Tokyo and to the Allied firebomb attacks on the Japanese islands in World War II. The earliest anime were probably the work of Oten Shimokawa, a political cartoonist for the *Tokyo Puck* magazine. In 1917 Shimokawa experimented with several short animated films (none of which survive) in which he drew characters in white lines on a blackboard, filmed the drawing for one or two frames, altered the drawing and filmed it again, and so forth. He also tried drawing directly onto film. Around the same time another artist named Seitaro Kitayama created anime based on Japanese fairy tales and legends as well as animated commercials and educational films. Kitayama also started Japan's first animation studio, a project that was abandoned when he left the medium to make live-action newsreels.

The oldest surviving anime were produced in the year following the Tokyo earthquake by Kitayama's apprentice, Sanae Yamamoto. These works include *Obasuteyama* (*The Mountain Where Old Women Are Abandoned*) and *Usagi to Kame* (*The Tortoise and the Hare*). They were designed for accompaniment by music and a spoken narration, like other early silent films in Japan. The first anime with sound was Noburo Ofuji's *Kujira* (*Whale*) of 1927, a film of animated silhouettes synchronized to the *William Tell Overture*. Ofuji went on to create *Kuro Nyago* (*Black Cat*), in which two felines shimmied to jazz, and the first color anime, *Ogon no Hana* (*Golden Flower*). Innovative anime like these were screened not only at cinemas but also in shops and schools. For example, students learned consideration for others in 1929's *Taro-san no Kisha* (*Taro's Steamtrain*), in which a Japanese boy struggles to keep order among rowdy, humanlike animals in a train carriage.

Tokyo's main shopping district shows extensive damage after the 1923 Great Kanto earthquake. Few examples of early Japanese animation exist today because of the earthquake and because of Allied firebombing during World War II.

The word *anime*, based on the English word *animation*, originated with film critic Taihei Imamura in his 1948 book *Manga Eigaron* (*On Animated Films*). This sort of coining is typical of the way foreign words are absorbed into the Japanese language. Anime has come to refer to Japanese animation in particular, although in Japan it includes animation from anywhere in the world.

Techniques of Early Anime

The first animated images were created with a succession of drawings. A child can animate a stick figure on a drawing pad by varying the position of the arms and legs slightly for each drawing and then flipping the pages to create the illusion of motion. Early animators used a process called stop-motion cinematography that was similar to the child's flicking-book approach. Hand-drawn frames were photographed in sequence and then projected at twenty-four frames a second to bring the illustrator's static art into motion.

Early anime in Japan generally followed the procedures used by Western animators such as Walt Disney and the Fleischer brothers in their Hollywood cartoons. For example, like them, Japanese animators began to use celluloid animation, or cel animation, in order to work more rapidly. In the earliest cartoons the background was redrawn for each frame—a very time-consuming process. Animators soon discovered a better approach: drawing characters on transparent celluloid and laying the drawings over a background image that does not change for seconds or minutes at a time. This practical method quickly became universal.

As the technique progressed, different parts of an image were drawn or painted on different layers of celluloid. This not only allowed the animator to reuse a background repeatedly as characters moved in front of it. The contrast between the shading of a background and the vivid lines or colors of a character in the foreground also created a sense of depth. To get this effect, artists began to use an animation stand. This device enabled them to stack layers of painted celluloid inches apart and place a camera above the stack to film through the layers. Anime historian Thomas LaMarre connects this process to earlier Japanese graphic art. He explains, "Considered from the angle of art, such a use of layers feels more compatible with the layering techniques associated with Japanese wood block prints (ukiyo-e) of the Edo period, in which printers stamped various layers of color onto paper. . . . This is surely one of the reasons why many commentators turn to Edo prints as a predecessor for anime."[12] LaMarre also points out that Japanese animators such as Kimura Hakusan were working with sophisticated animation stands in the early 1930s.

Full Animation and Limited Animation

Around the same time, Disney, frustrated by his cartoons' lack of financial success, was seeking even more realistic effects. He began to work on introducing the illusion of moving into depth—as in a tracking shot when a character seems to approach a house that gets increasingly larger and blocks out other objects in the field of vision.

Disney solved the problem by creating a multiplane camera that constantly adjusts the proportional relations between the different layers of the image. For the viewer, the world and the characters presented in the animation are constantly in scale and in proper proportion. Disney patented his invention in 1940. One year later Mitsuyo Seo's *Ari-chan* (*Little Ant*) was the first Japanese animated cartoon to use the multiplane camera. This system remained the chief means of conveying depth of field until the 1990s.

Disney's feature-length cartoons employed full animation, which mimicked the fluid movement of live-action cinema. In general, however, Japanese anime uses limited animation, which relies on other effects—and many fewer drawings—to portray depth and movement. For example, a pilot at the controls of a biplane might be shown in the exact same position for several successive shots, with only his hair blowing to give an illusion of motion. Limited animation is much less expensive to produce, allowing for tremendous growth in anime production. Defenders of this technique also insist that it focuses more attention on plot, voice acting, and overall composition. Nevertheless, compared to the flow of Disney-style full animation and modern computer animation, most anime can appear rather clunky and static.

Anime as a Propaganda Tool

Despite its static, two-dimensional presentation, anime became a powerful tool for propaganda during the 1930s and early 1940s. Japan's militaristic government used anime to spread its message of Japanese aggression and dominance to the people. Animators received public funding and national distribution for their propaganda films. One of the first propaganda anime was Yasuji Murata's *Sora no Momotarō* (*Aerial Momotaro*) in 1931. In the film Momotaro (or Peach Boy), a hero from Japanese folklore, pilots an aircraft to a remote island near

Unlike Disney's fully animated scenes that attempt to mimic real-world motion, anime generally relies on limited animation and fewer drawings to depict depth and movement. Some people think this style is clunky and static.

the South Pole, where he breaks up a conflict between penguins and albatrosses. Japanese audiences did not fail to recognize the parallels with Japan's recent invasion of Manchuria in retaliation for alleged Chinese military attacks on the Japanese-owned railroad there. Yoshitaro Kataoka's *Bandanemon the Monster Exterminator* introduced another Japanese tough guy who saved villagers from an influx of tanuki, or shape-shifting creatures—posing as beautiful sexpots like the animated American character Betty Boop.

When Japan's invasion of Manchuria drew condemnation from the League of Nations and the world's democracies, its animators were directed to attack foreign powers in their films. In 1933 Takao Nakano made *Kuroneko Banzai* (*Black Cat Banzai*) in which malevolent batlike bombers piloted by Mickey Mouse look-alikes attack

A Tantalizing Snippet

Every nation tends to promote its culture as original and innovative. With anime such an important part of Japanese culture, it is not surprising that there should be keen interest about the very first example of Japanese animation. In late 2005 Natsuki Matsumoto, a lecturer at Osaka University, discovered an old piece of 35 millimeter film stock in a projector inside a Kyoto residence. The snippet, only fifty frames in length, lasts three seconds. It depicts a boy in a sailor suit painting the Chinese characters for "moving pictures" on a blackboard and then doffing his cap. The drawings were made in red and black directly onto the film. Matsumoto could not determine who drew the anime, when it was made, nor even if it had ever been shown. Judging strictly by the technique, Matsumoto speculated that it was made around 1907—fully a decade before the first Japanese anime supposedly appeared. This led some to claim that the world's first animation had arisen in Japan without Western influence. While Matsumoto's find is intriguing, experts still disagree about its true age.

an innocent parade of toys. During World War II the imperial navy commissioned Mitsuyo Seo to bring back Momotaro in *Momotarō no Umiwashi* (*Momotaro's Sea Eagles*), a thirty-seven-minute smash hit that presented a "united" Asian naval force composed of cute animals attacking an enemy base similar to Pearl Harbor. Wartime rationing brought new challenges to anime production. According to anime encyclopedists Jonathan Clements and Helen McCarthy, "With animation cels in short supply (nitro-cellulose was a crucial ingredient in gunpowder), Seo's animators were forced to wash their materials in acid and reuse them for this tale of the bombing of Pearl Harbor in fairy-tale form, destroying the original artwork even as they shot each frame of animation."[13] Seo produced an even more successful sequel called *Momotarō: Umi no Shinpei* (*Momotaro's Divine Sea Warriors*), the first full-length anime feature, which presented the Peach Boy leading an army of monkeys, rabbits, and other animals to fend off a British invasion force. However, these portrayals of Japanese triumphs were overtaken by actual events, including the atomic bombs dropped on Hiroshima and Nagasaki in 1945 that led to Japan's surrender.

Toei Doga, the First Anime Studio

Japan's defeat left the country economically crippled and occupied by American forces. Production of new anime virtually stopped. The few new films produced were fantasies or sentimental stories that reinforced Western-style values or focused on old Japanese cultural traditions. For example, Masao Kumagawa's *Maho no Pen* (*The Magic Pen*) is a magical tale about an orphan boy who discovers a doll with a magic pen that can conjure food and shelter in the form of an American-style house. Independent anime creators continued to make the occasional artistic film throughout the 1950s, including Ofuji's celebrated reworking of *The Whale* using colored silhouettes. However, as the Japanese economy recovered, the first commercial anime studio arose. Founded in 1956, Toei Doga, as it was called, drew upon the Japanese population's love of Disney cartoons and set its sights on challenging Disney as an animation leader. Toei's first feature, called *Hakujaden* (*Panda and the Magic Serpent*), employed the Disney formula of cute animals that sang and danced. Later features were based on Japanese legends and adventure tales, with heroes that had funny animals as companions. These films provided a number of future directors and artists with invaluable experience and also led to the creation of other anime studios.

Osamu Tezuka and Anime on TV

One of the artists who collaborated with Toei was the manga master Osamu Tezuka. The 1960 Toei film *Saiyuki* (*Alakazam the Great*) was based on Tezuka's manga retelling of the Monkey King legend from ancient China. Intrigued by anime's possibilities, Tezuka started his own studio, Mushi Productions, in 1961. His first project was a prize-winning experimental film with an antiwar theme called *Aru Machikado no Monogatari* (*Tale of a Street Corner*). But Tezuka wanted to reach a wider audience. Impressed with the new Hanna-Barbera cartoons from America, with their cheaply produced limited animation, Tezuka imagined using that technique for a wide range of modern stories based on the different genres found in manga. These series would be ideal for television, which was just coming into its own in Japan, particularly in preparation for the 1964 Tokyo Olympic Games.

Tezuka's first anime series for television was based on his popular manga series *Tetsuwan Atom* (*Mighty Atom*) about the robot boy with an atomic heart who can never grow up. As anime writer Gilles Poitras observes, "In *Tetsuwan Atom* we see a thematic motif that turns up again and again in Japan: the doll with a soul. In the West we have the Pinocchio story, but in Japan there is the added element, from an old folk belief, that a doll loved and cared for could develop an actual soul."[14] The series debuted on Japan's Fuji TV on New Year's Day 1963 and was an immediate sensation. Tezuka claimed that American television inquired about the rights only a few days later. NBC secured the rights and provided Mushi Productions with cash to spiff up the animation with more cels. NBC then sold the series into syndication, meaning that local stations paid to broadcast it. Since the translated title *Mighty Atom* was much like the name of a DC Comics superhero, American producer Fred Ladd retitled the series *Astro Boy*. The anime about the little robot hero quickly became a hit not only in the United States but worldwide.

Tezuka and his staff at Mushi Productions discovered that in order to deliver *Tetsuwan Atom* episodes on time and within the budget, they had to find ways to cut corners. Mushi artists have testified to working overtime with blistered and bleeding fingers and sleeping at their desks to meet deadlines. Yet their new techniques for producing limited animation soon became the industry standard. For example, they employed as few as eight drawings for the twenty-four film

Astro Boy (pictured in a mural in Tokyo) became a hit television series in the United States shortly after it debuted on Japanese television as *Tetsuwan Atom* (*Mighty Atom*) in 1963. The futuristic adventures of the little robot hero appealed to fans worldwide.

frames that run through a projector per second, resulting in jerky or even static animation. (At least twelve drawings are required for more fluid animation to rival live-action filming.) To give the impression of higher quality animation, more drawings per second were used for

The Artfulness of *Kimba*

For a children's cartoon show with cute animal characters, Osamu Tezuka's *Kimba the White Lion* was uncommonly artful. To begin with, the series did not shy away from life's complexity. In the very first episode both of Kimba's parents die tragic deaths, his father from a hunter's bullet and his mother by drowning in a storm at sea. As Kimba swims back to the jungle, he sees his mother's silhouette as a constellation in the violet night sky and becomes aware of the approaching shore when he notices a swarm of multicolored butterflies. Details like these showed Tezuka's determination to raise anime to an art form. The series' overall theme of bringing peace to the jungle and living harmoniously with other creatures was also unusual for an animated production.

The artfulness of Tezuka's *Kimba* apparently was not lost on the creative team at Disney Studios. As Jonathan Clements and Helen McCarthy relate, "The series had slowly faded from public perception until the release of Disney's *The Lion King* (1994), the tale of a lion called Simba, whose father dies, who just can't wait to be king, who has a mandrill for a counselor, an argumentative parrot-like bird (a hornbill) for a friend, and an evil, scarred lion adversary (plus bumbling hyena minions)." All these elements are similar to *Kimba*, yet Disney's team insisted they were unaware of Tezuka's series. Many observers have suggested that Tezuka would have seen *The Lion King* as a fitting tribute to his work.

Jonathan Clements and Helen McCarthy, *The Anime Encyclopedia: Revised and Expanded Edition*. Berkeley: Stonebridge, 2006, p. 339.

one or two important scenes per episode. Mushi animators also used tricks to reduce work, such as panning across an image or zooming in with the camera to suggest movement. They focused on close-ups or character groupings for several seconds at a time. They created a bank of images that could be reused again and again, including loops of animation such as Astro Boy rocketing off into the air. Voice tracks were added after the characters were drawn, and the dialogue was spoken to match the image. With foreign audiences in mind, animators also cut out Japanese references, such as characters eating with chopsticks or visiting a Shinto shrine. Excessively violent images were also deleted. Despite the sometimes primitive-looking results, fans returned to their TV screens each week to watch the futuristic adventures of Astro Boy.

The Anime Market Expands

Mushi Productions' success with overseas audiences brought new competitors into the field. In 1963 Ladd bought the rights to fifty-two episodes of an anime series about a giant radio-controlled robot called *Tetsujin 28-Go*. Ladd renamed the robot and the series *Gigantor* and added theme music and character details aimed at the American market. For example, the young boy who controlled Gigantor was called Jimmy Sparks, and one early villain was Dr. Katzmeow.

This first animated foray into the giant robot genre, or mecha, would influence later series from *Transformers* to *Mobile Suit Gundam*. Other action series followed, including *Marine Boy*, about an amphibious youngster with a pet dolphin and a mermaid girlfriend, and the aforementioned *Speed Racer*. Milder fantasy series also met with success. *Little Witch Sally*, the first anime based on shojo manga and the first

> **Words in Context**
> *panning*
> Moving the motion picture camera across an image to keep a character or object in sight or in focus.

in a long line of "magical girl" anime, follows a young princess who leaves the Land of Magic to live among humans and help them secretly with her magic powers. This series, running from 1966 to 1967, was inspired by the American TV show *Bewitched*, indicating how cultural influences bounced back and forth between Japan and the West. Tezuka's Mushi Productions scored a major hit with the stylish *Kimba the White Lion*, which was the first full-color anime series and is based on Tezuka's *Jungle Taitei* manga. Tezuka also adapted his

1950s magical-girl classic *Ribon no Kishi* to make *Princess Knight*, another landmark series, in 1967. With his remarkable creative energy, Tezuka influenced anime production just as decisively as he did the field of manga. His work also reveals how manga and anime were successfully overlapping and creating a market for Japanese cartoon art overseas.

Chapter Four

Anime's Worldwide Success

The number of anime series produced in Japan and finding audiences in the United States and around the world has been like a tsunami, or huge tidal wave. This wave is reflected in the title for the Cartoon Network's original block of anime programming: Toonami. Beginning on March 17, 1997, the network began presenting a Saturday night block of action-oriented animation made up mostly of classic anime series including *Dragon Ball Z*, *Gundam Wing*, *One Piece*, and *Naruto*. This was many American fans' first exposure to more sophisticated anime. Toonami proved enormously popular and was a regular feature on the network until 2008. Besides regular series, there were special events such as Giant Robot Week, devoted to mecha anime, and A Month of Miyazaki, focusing on acclaimed director Hayao Miyazaki's works. Anime fan and blogger mustang87 expresses most viewers' excitement. "Toonami was probably the greatest block of shows ever in Cartoon Network history," the blogger writes. "This is what probably got most anime fans started (including myself). I actually think back to all the violent, action-filled shows and think 'Wow. My parents actually let me watch this stuff.'"[15] After a four-year hiatus Toonami returned to the Cartoon Network in 2012. It remains a good source for sampling a variety of today's cutting-edge anime.

In 1997 the Cartoon Network began featuring a Saturday-night block of action-oriented animation made up mostly of classic anime series such as *One Piece* and *Dragon Ball Z* (pictured). The enormously popular group of shows went by the name Toonami.

Anime in Outer Space

Despite a shaky beginning, the 1970s became the formative years for more cutting-edge anime, particularly in the genre of space-age adventures. Osamu Tezuka's Mushi Productions, after releasing adult-oriented features such as *Senya Ichiya Monogatari* (*Arabian Nights*) and *Cleopatra*, finally went bankrupt and closed down in 1973. Toei Studios abandoned elaborate feature-length animation in favor of cheaper TV productions. Overall the Japanese market for anime seemed stuck in the doldrums, with few bright spots. One of these was a series about a master thief created by the manga artist known as Monkey Punch. *Lupin Sansei*, with its sophisticated jet-set background and mixture of adult humor and wild violence, was aimed squarely at older audiences and grew so popular that it spawned two sequel series and some feature films. Its main contribution, however, was in demonstrating anime's potential appeal for adult viewers. This enabled the science-fiction series that followed to pursue more sophisticated themes and plot lines. Anime was no longer considered amusement for children.

One of the best of the new series was *Uchu Senkan Yamato* (*Space Battleship Yamato*), a gritty, violent science-fiction saga about a spaceship crew battling to save humanity from an alien invasion. Created by several artists who worked together at Mushi Productions, including the decade's rising star Leiji Matsumoto, the series thrilled Japanese audiences by transposing World War II–style naval and aerial battles into a space-age setting. The plot has the crew refitting the hulk of the sunken battleship *Yamato* (an actual ship in the Imperial Navy) to fight the evil emperor Desslar and his minions. While the show included preposterous physics—spacecraft plummet after being blasted, even though there is no "down" in outer space—its story lines were always strong, with complex character development. "The influence of the original series on a whole generation of Japanese animators is incredible," write anime experts Jonathan Clements and Helen McCarthy, "and it resulted in homages [tributes] and cameos for the ship in many anime works."[16] Under the title *Star Blazers*, the show also made its mark on American viewers beginning in 1979, drawing impetus from the then-recent success of *Star Wars*.

Space Battleship Yamato showed the way for other new science-fiction series, particularly giant robot shows such as *Gatchaman* and *Kido Senshi Gundam* (*Mobile Suit Gundam*). *Gatchaman*, known in the United States as *Battle of the Planets*, features the Science Ninja Team struggling to defeat the evil Galactor forces and their gigantic robots. The American version was so heavily edited for violence that a silly robot character was added to offset the missing footage. *Mobile Suit Gundam*, with its echoes of Go Nagai's *Mazinger Z* (also an anime hit) and the earlier and more juvenile *Gigantor*, follows fifteen-year-old Amuro Ray as he and his comrades battle enemy soldiers in mechanized "mobile suits" that are like huge piloted robots. The show combined the thrills of the giant robot genre with sprawling plot lines and nuanced characters. "A central theme of *Gundam* is that of civilians caught up in war doing the best they can in difficult or deadly situations,"[17] writes Gilles Poitras. Like other new series, *Gundam* also explored moral dilemmas and emotional extremes once considered too sophisticated for cartoons. *Gundam* proved to be an enduring franchise in Japan, with many sequels, spinoffs, and movies as well as merchandising of action figures and model kits.

Home Video and the Golden Age

For all their innovations, *Yamato*, *Gundam*, and the other space operas were only the beginning of anime's rise. Developments in the 1980s ushered in what many anime fans consider to be the medium's golden age. Certainly one of the most important developments was the introduction of Original Video Anime (OVA), or anime made to be released on videocassette. With the first OVA release in 1983 anime distribution changed forever. Producers no longer had to arrange for theatrical release or secure a TV time slot for their anime. More experimental series could be marketed directly to fans and remained available in catalogs and on store shelves for years after their creation. Plotlines could be condensed to a preplanned number of episodes, like the chapters in a novel, or could sprawl over as many episodes as fans were willing to buy. Among the series that benefited from the new format were cyperpunk offerings such as the eight-episode *Bubblegum Crisis*, with its all-female mercenary team called the Knight Sabers, and Katsuhiro Otomo's dark, post-apocalyptic classic *Akira*. The latter, with its focus on a dysfunctional future that resembled the world of the 1982 live-action film *Blade Runner*, was a huge hit and demonstrated anime's appeal to adult viewers worldwide. The freedom from censorship offered by OVA release also started a flood of sexually explicit anime, called *hentai*. Go Nagai's *Kekko Kamen*, about a masked superheroine who fights against fiendish schoolmasters and happens to be mostly naked, was one of the tamer entries in this line.

> **Words in Context**
> *Original Video Anime (OVA)*
> Anime specifically created to be released on videocassette.

To keep up with the demand for new anime, producers began to adapt the most popular manga, as with Akira Toriyama's kung fu fantasy *Dragon Ball* and Rumiko Takahashi's romantic comedy *Maison Ikkoku*. Anime tailored to sports fans, history buffs, video game enthusiasts, and younger viewers also thrived. Producers even had success with anime based on literary classics such as *The Tale of Genji*.

The New Studios

Growth in anime production convinced talented creators to join together to form new studios. Studio Gainax was founded in 1984 by a group

Voice Acting in Anime

Voice acting—or *seiyu* in Japanese—adds personality and emotional depth to the characters. Voices for anime are added after the animation is complete, which is the reverse of the process in other countries. This allows anime voice actors to tailor their performances to nuances on the screen. Many anime voice actors also dub voices for the large number of imported films and TV series in Japan. As a result, dozens of voice-acting schools have arisen to meet the demand. Japanese voice actors known for doing the voices of particular Western movie stars are employed by shrewd producers to voice similar characters in anime, adding a certain Hollywood luster to the proceedings. In turn, some Hollywood stars such as Patrick Stewart, Kirsten Dunst, and Claire Danes have done the English voices for Studio Ghibli's productions.

With anime fandom so obsessive about their favorite series, the best voice actors—most of them women—often become stars. The most celebrated voice actor is a former nurse named Megumi Hayashibara, who has parlayed her amazing success into a second career as a pop singer and songwriter. Hayashibara's voice-acting resume reads like a history of anime's greatest hits. Known as the Woman of a Thousand Voices, this hardworking actor has played Dr. Atsuko "Paprika" Chiba in *Paprika*, Faye Valentine in *Cowboy Bebop*, Momoko Sakurayama in *Patlabor*, and Rei Ayanami and the penguin Pen Pen in *Neon Genesis Evangelion*. Hayashibara is so well known that one anime character was actually based on her.

of lower-level animators and anime fans determined to make their mark in the industry with more inventive visuals and storylines. Chief among these creative minds was Hideaki Anno, whose wry humor and willingness to experiment led to such anime classics as *Gunbuster*, *Nadia: Secret of Blue Water*, and particularly *Neon Genesis Evangelion*. With its alien invasion, giant robots, and references to World War II, *Evangelion* used the staples of anime science fiction to present a kaleidoscopic saga that was part parody and part intellectual essay. Despite its whiny lead character and plotlines that became more perplexing as the series went on, *Evangelion* held its fans with beautifully detailed artwork and cultural references to everything from the Book of Revelation to the Austrian psychotherapist Sigmund Freud. Also typical of a Gainax production was the series' lack of money at the end. The final two episodes had to be assembled from a mishmash of previous clips (explained as a look into the main character's psyche). Reportedly Anno received death threats from fans who were outraged at the shoddy results.

In 1985 an even more important anime studio opened its doors: Studio Ghibli. Its founders were Hayao Miyazaki and Isao Taka-

The celebrated anime director Hayao Miyazaki talks to reporters at Studio Ghibli in 2014. The studio's founding in 1985 made it possible for Miyazaki and others to create many enchanting anime films.

hata, soon to become two of the most celebrated directors in anime. Their decision to form Ghibli followed their team's success with Miyazaki's *Nausicaä of the Valley of the Wind*. This lovely film told the story of a young princess, Nausicaä, who fights to save her people and the world from human enemies and ecological disaster. Scenes of Nausicaä soaring in the sky on her personal glider were typical of Miyazaki's love of aviation and sense of visual grandeur. Encouraged by the reaction to *Nausicaä*, Miyasaki and Takahata formed a historic partnership with the producer Toshio Suzuki, the former editor of *Animage* magazine. According to Suzuki, the studio's name was significant: "For the name, we brainstormed a lot, looking for a Japanese word. One day, Miyazaki said, 'How about Ghibli?' A nickname for an Italian spy plane. Originally, it's a word for the hot wind that blows through the Sahara. He said, 'We're about to blow a new wind through the animation world, you know?' So that's how we decided on that name."[18]

Miyazaki's Mastery

The main creative force behind this new wind was Miyazaki. Born on the outskirts of Tokyo in 1941, Miyazaki grew up fascinated with manga, although his own drawing skill was slow to develop. He loved Osamu Tezuka's work best of all, but early on he decided to forge his own path. After studying economics and political science in college, he got a job at Toei Animation and became friends with Takahata. Despite a growing reputation in the industry, Miyazaki grew frustrated at the limited budgets and frenzied schedules for TV anime. He longed to do more expressive animation in a feature film. In 1979 he finally got his chance to direct a full-length anime, a charming spy thriller called *Castle of Cagliostro*, which starred Monkey Punch's Lupin character. Four years later he made *Nausicaä* and never looked back. (Always full of creative energy, Miyazaki also completed a much more involved manga version of *Nausicaä*, showing his continued love of the manga form.) Miyazaki's first film for Studio Ghibli was *Castle in the Sky*, a fantasy adventure about flying cities and sky pirates with echoes of old-fashioned Hollywood heroics. One particular image, of the girl Sheeta floating down through the power of her glowing blue pendant into the waiting arms of the young mineworker Pazu, encapsulates Miyazaki's ability to enchant an audience. However, it was a 1988 film for Studio Ghibli that truly established his place as a master of anime. *My Neighbor Totoro*, a child's fantasy set in the countryside of 1950s Japan, follows two young sisters as they discover a host of magical creatures, including the furry balloon-like, forest spirit Totoro. Drawing upon childhood memories of his own mother's battle with tuberculosis, Miyazaki manages to see the world through the eyes of four-year-old Mei and her older sister, Satsuki, whose mother is confined to a clinic. The film's gorgeous visual details of forest, fields, and changing weather set new standards for anime. Fans of the film still love to visit the landscapes outside Tokyo that Miyazaki used as the basis for his drawings, and seemingly every Japanese home contains a stuffed version of Totoro.

For a double feature with *Totoro*, Takahata offered his own classic *Grave of the Fireflies*, about young victims of World War II who try to survive in the ruins of Kobe after the city has been firebombed by American planes. Fans and industry observers alike were astonished at the quality of the new studio's output. Helen McCarthy declares that Studio Ghibli "has earned a reputation for an attention to detail and quality in every aspect of a production that borders on

the fanatical: Miyazaki is one of the few directors in the industry who personally checks every key frame and redraws any he doesn't find suitable, a task most leave to the senior animators."[19] The method was exhausting, but the results made it all worthwhile. Later Miyazaki films from Ghibli include *Princess Mononoke*, an environmental parable that is perhaps his greatest overall achievement, and the Oscar-winning *Spirited Away*. Today Miyazaki towers over anime the way Tezuka did in the field of manga. One of the greatest tributes to Miyazaki came from John Lasseter, founder of Pixar, the American studio responsible for *Finding Nemo*, *The Incredibles*, and *Wall-E*. "At Pixar," Lasseter says, "when we have a problem and we can't seem to solve it, we often take a laser disc of one of Miyazaki's films and look at a scene

Pixar founder John Lasseter (pictured with the Buzz Lightyear character from the company's delightful *Toy Story* movies) says those movies were inspired by the imaginative anime of Hayao Miyazaki.

in our screening room for a shot of inspiration and it always works! We come away amazed and inspired. *Toy Story* owes a huge debt of gratitude to the films of Miyazaki."[20]

Computer Animation to the Rescue

While Miyazaki and Ghibli dominated feature-length anime throughout the 1990s and into the new century, imaginative work continued to appear in made-for-TV series and straight-to-video offerings. To meet the steady demand for product, companies increasingly turned to more efficient computer animation. In the past, when all animation was done by hand, a director or team of artists prepared storyboards with sketches of the action for each scene. Then a senior key animator used the storyboards to create the layouts, or basic drawings for each scene. Finally a team of key animators drew the key frames—the main drawings that begin and end each action or motion. The job of connecting the key frames with a series of drawings to make a movement look natural was done by an inbetweener—an apprentice artist working usually for minimal pay. Most of the inbetweener's work now is performed using a computer program that fills in the connecting drawings automatically. Original sketches can be drawn and manipulated with a mechanical pen using a program such as Photoshop. Computers are also used to paint animation cels more rapidly with digital ink and to perform the compositing process, which is how the images are transferred to film.

With the anime industry numbering more than four hundred production studios today and accounting for the majority of DVD sales in Japan, the drive for production shortcuts is relentless. Advances in digital animation continue to streamline the process, enabling animators to perform much of their work on computer screens rather than with pen and paper. Also, animation in Japan generally has a greater focus on art quality than on movement. Thus, the detail of lush or complex backgrounds is more important to anime fans than the fluid movement found in Hollywood-style animation.

Anime's Continuing Popularity

Studio Ghibli's success led other studios to experiment recklessly with high-budget anime that ended up losing money. This along with an economic downturn in Japan caused many studios to close and brought an end to anime's so-called golden age. Some studios such as Gainax began to focus on TV series once more. In the last two decades a steady stream of imaginative series in every conceivable genre has continued to appear. As viewers outside Japan have become more sophisticated, they have embraced the intricate and deceptive plot twists, savage humor, and teeming cultural references that are found in the most cutting-edge anime. A short series like Fuminori Kizaki's *Afro Samurai* includes the voice of actor and anime fan

A Promising Debut

Living up to the successes of Studio Ghibli's founders, Hiyao Miyazaki and Isao Takahata, can be a bit intimidating for a first-time director. Yet judging by the beautiful 2010 release *The Secret World of Arrietty*, Hiromasa Yonebayashi has what it takes to continue the studio's artistic dominance. Yonebayashi studied industrial design at an art college before joining Ghibli as a junior animator. His work on such films as *Princess Mononoke* led to his promotion to key animator. He then directed two short films for the Studio Ghibli art museum before finally earning his first feature film assignment. Miyazaki and Takahata had long considered doing a version of Mary Norton's novel *The Borrowers*. They told Yonebayashi to read the book and prepare storyboards. The first-time director was charmed by the story, and he immediately began to sketch prospective scenes. However, Yonebayashi's original vision for the film was too dark for Miyazaki. "At first, I had taken the story in a more serious direction by highlighting the struggles and survival of a dying species of little people, but Miyazaki didn't approve it," recalls Yonebayashi. "As we continued to flesh out the story, Miyazaki suggested that we go in another direction, and after several conversations, we settled on something more wistful, focusing on the relationship between a boy and girl." The change proved sound at the box office. *The Secret World of Arrietty* was the highest grossing Japanese film of 2010.

Quoted in *The Art of The Secret World of Arrietty*. San Francisco: VIZ Media, LLC, 2012.

Samuel Jackson and features ultrahip characters listening to hip-hop on their cell phones and engaging in samurai sword fights. The wacky saga *One Piece* follows a rubber-limbed hero named Monkey D. Luffy who battles pirates while searching for a fabled treasure. Akiyuki

Shinbo's *Monogatari* combines magical-girl pizzazz with demons, ghosts, and vampires. The atmospheric *Attack on Titan* employs a familiar humanity-on-the-brink storyline in original ways. Seemingly any combination of genres and themes has the potential to be a hit anime. It all depends on the right director and a creative team attuned to his or her vision. However, it is the global audience that will ensure the survival and appreciation of anime and its print-based forerunner, manga. These two art forms now have their own sections in bookstores and movie markets throughout the world, signaling their widespread appeal and their continuing economic viability.

Chapter Five

Anime and Manga: Fans and Future Prospects

In January of 2014 the official website of the *Pretty Guardian Sailor Moon* franchise announced an upcoming remake of the popular twenty-year-old anime series. Creator Naoko Takeuchi said that the new version of the story, about a team of girls dressed in sailor suits and endowed with magical powers, would follow the original manga more closely. "With precious little info released over the past year," writes entertainment reporter Michael Mammano, "fans have been speculating desperately about every aspect of this new project. What would it mean to the franchise and fandom? Would it add to the original's legacy or detract from it, and to what degree?"[21] Such breathless enthusiasm among fans is ripe for exploitation by marketers. *Sailor Moon* is a good example of how the most popular anime and manga become merchandising bonanzas. Besides DVDs and comics, the *Sailor Moon* franchise has produced live-action series, video games, stage musicals, art books, action figures, compact mirrors, chopsticks, and even lingerie. The new series will be available on a Japanese streaming video service and probably will be sold to the

> **Words in Context**
> *fandom*
> All the fans of manga or anime considered as a group.

Two young women model their *Sailor Moon* costumes at a Japanese comics show. Popular anime and manga stories have become merchandizing bonanzas, with live-action series, video games, action figures, costumes, and more.

Cartoon Network for inclusion in its Toonami lineup. With their rabid fan bases, blockbuster anime and manga like *Sailor Moon* continue to impact pop culture not only in Japan but around the world.

Do-It-Yourself Manga

One indication of just how dedicated manga fans can be is the rapid growth of *dojinshi*, or manga produced by readers. The manga boom of the 1990s saw magazines such as *Shonen Jump* selling six million copies a week and fans spending hours at manga cafes, where they could sip drinks and sample manga at leisure. Some imaginative fans began to create their own manga, employing the distinctive style of their favorite artists and often using actual characters from popular manga in new stories. Despite their violation of Japanese copyright laws, these *dojinshi* met with little opposition from publishers. For one thing, *dojinshi* artists—called *dojinshika*—tended to be the most rabid and dependable purchasers of manga, and publishers were cautious about alienating them. In addition publishers saw *dojinshi* as free publicity for their regular titles. Much *dojinshi* proved to be so professionally done that it was hard to distinguish from the genuine article. Some publishers began to troll these amateur publications for fresh ideas or potential new artists. Several successful artists got their start doing *dojinshi*, and some established artists have turned to the form to try out controversial themes or plots.

As the trend continued, well-stocked shops appeared that catered to fans of *dojinshi*. Popular amateur artists developed followings that many professionals would envy. *Dojinshi* conventions became huge attractions, drawing tens of thousands of visitors. Many *dojinshi*, including Yoshitoshi Abe's *Haibane Renmei*, have been made into successful anime.

Inevitably, the lack of publishers' control over *dojinshi* has enabled many of the amateur artists to dabble in pornography. Artists and fans alike seem to enjoy the spectacle of popular characters being placed in compromising situations. While much of this material is merely bawdy, it also reflects the Japanese acceptance of quite explicit sex and violence in manga and anime.

The *Pokémon* Phenomenon

At the other end of the spectrum from explicit offerings aimed at adults are the cuddly creatures of *Pokémon*. The name is a shortened version of the Japanese title "Pocket Monsters." *Pokémon* began in 1996 as a computer game based on the idea of collecting and cataloging species, like a naturalist, a pastime that creator Satoshi Tajiri loved as a child. Tajiri designed a game in which players capture and train the tiny creatures to wage battles with those of other players. As the franchise has expanded, 718 different fictional species of Pokémon have been identified, and the game has gone through six separate generations with new characters and playing strategies. It is the second-best-selling video game franchise of all time.

The *Pokémon* craze soon spun off manga and anime aimed at young fans. In the *Pokémon* anime series, a trainer named Satoshi (or Ash Ketchum in the American version) goes on a quest to find Pokémon, accompanied by his first capture, a chubby, yellow, rodentlike creature named Pikachu, and a small band of friends. The anime, like the game, emphasizes the idea of adventure and personal mastery. *Pokémon* expert Patricia Hernandez describes the franchise's appeal to young players and readers: "But wherever you went, there it was. *Pokémon*. Even then, during the late 90s, it wasn't too hard to see why. Here's this franchise about kids who go on adventures to become 'Pokémon masters,' and in practice what that really means is that you can leave home when you're like 8 years old to see the world with your friends and pets. Pretty seductive, as a fantasy. (And highly lucrative, as merchandise.)"[22] Introduced in the United States in 1998, *Pokémon* has gone on to capture a worldwide audience. Its games, comic books, film, toys, and trading cards have made billions of dollars for the owner of the franchise, Nintendo.

Otaku and the Rise of Fan Conventions

Pokémon's dedicated fans are just one example of *otaku*, the most obsessive consumers of manga and anime. The word *otaku* means "you" and is generally used as a polite form of address between strangers—such as the manga and anime enthusiasts who meet at comics shops, video stores, manga cafes, and fan conventions. To a Japanese, the word carries some of the same associations as the English slang words *geek* or *nerd*, but with even more negative ideas of obsession and social ineptitude. Supposedly the production staff of the 1982 anime series *Super Dimension Fortress Macross* began using the word to refer to the polite but painfully shy fans

The *Pokémon* craze began as a computer game in which players capture and train tiny creatures to wage battles with those of other players. It has expanded to include an anime television series and a whole array of toys, trading cards, and games.

they met at conventions. Where *otaku* used to refer to males almost exclusively, a growing number of females fit the description. The character of the awkward but well-informed *otaku* is now a staple of manga and anime. Fans in other countries have cheerfully adopted the name for themselves and use it in the titles of fan-based magazines and websites.

Conventions where *otaku* and more casual fans can meet to discuss and trade their favorite manga and anime have exploded in popularity not only in Japan but worldwide. For example, Comiket, a gathering held twice a year in Tokyo, was started by a circle of friends who wanted to buy and sell *dojinshi*, the self-published manga. While the first Comiket in 1975 drew about seven hundred attendees, today's shows regularly attract a half million fans. Many anime or manga conventions in Japan are sponsored by studios or publishers seeking to promote their latest products. Conventions often feature screenings of new and classic anime, appearances by popular directors, artists, or voice actors, panel discussions about the state of anime art, and loads of merchandise related to various anime franchises. Conventions are also the perfect backdrop for *cosplay*, which is short for "costume play." This is a sort of performance art in which fans dress up as their favorite characters from manga, anime, or video games. Some go to great lengths to impress their fellow enthusiasts, spending hours making their costumes or paying hundreds of dollars for ready-made outfits. "For cosplayers," according to business writer Melia Robinson, "the experience is nearly always worth the stress of choosing a costume and dropping the dough. It's an opportunity to be a hero, princess, or otherworldly creature."[23]

Words in Context
dojinshi
Amateur manga produced by readers or fans.

An amusing look at *otaku* lifestyle is found in Takeshi Mori's half anime/half live-action *Otaku no Video* (*Fan's Video*). Loosely based on the true story of how Studio Gainax was founded, the film focuses on an ordinary young man who is coerced into joining an *otaku* circle, only to become so obsessed that he takes over the group as Otaking—the king of all *otaku*. The film spoofs everything from *otaku*'s obsessions with their anime heroes to the post-apocalyptic settings of so many anime. It even includes documentary-style interviews with actual fans, computer gamers, and cosplayers.

The Group Called CLAMP

One of the best examples of *dojinshi* artists' inspired amateurism is the all-female manga/anime group CLAMP. They began as a group of eleven in the mid-1980s, creating shojo manga featuring characters from popular series. Seven of the members moved to Tokyo and rented a small apartment for their work. In 1989 they went pro with *RG Veda*, a mythological saga. By 1993 the group had shrunk to its current lineup of four members: Nanase Ohkawa, who writes the stories and screenplays, and the artists Tsubaki Nekoi, Satsuki Igarashi, and Mokona. They began to create manga at a prodigious rate in many different genres, from the most lighthearted teenage romance to the goriest horror. As their manga have become popular, many have been translated for the overseas market.

A number of their manga have also been adapted by the group into equally successful anime, although usually with simplified plots and artwork.

CLAMP frequently have their characters crossover, or reappear in other series, a habit that dates from their playful *dojinshi* days. According to Ohkawa, this serves two purposes: "One is that readers get emotionally involved in the story quicker when a character they already know shows up, even if the plot isn't connected to the work they know the character from. The second is that it makes the characters feel more like real people—actors, if you will—than fictional characters."

Quoted in Dani Cavallaro, *CLAMP in Context: A Critical Study of the Manga and Anime*. McFarland, 2012, p. 8.

Breakthrough to American Culture

Fans of manga and anime in the United States have become just as fervent as their Japanese counterparts. The first attempts to bridge the cultural barrier between East and West with manga adaptations were only partially successful. In 1965 the American company Gold Key Comics published a version of Osamu Tezuka's *Astro Boy*—focusing on the TV series, not the manga. The stories were written and drawn by American artists who failed to provide the depth and wry humor of Tezuka's original work. A real breakthrough in the American market came in 1987 when First Comics put out a translated English edition of the popular *Lone Wolf and Cub* manga series about a swordsman and his son in medieval Japan. The US version features striking covers by the artist Frank Miller that helped attract American comic book fans. (Of course this version was "flopped," with the images reversed so that Americans could read them from left to right.) The entire series eventually appeared in English pocket-size editions by Dark Horse comics.

In 1989 Marvel Comics published a version of Katsuhiro Otomo's *Akira* that was not only translated and flopped but also colorized from the original Japanese black and white. With the success of *Akira*, a trickle of translated manga became a flood that has continued to this day. Another landmark event was Tokyopop's 2002 campaign boasting "100% Authentic Manga"—meaning the contents were not only in black and white but were also printed to be read from back to front and from right to left just like the original Japanese versions. This decision took into account the growing number of manga and anime fans ready to embrace the exotic nature of these genres. "No more flipped images! No more watered down manga!" announces one advertisement. "Imagine if Captain America suddenly started carrying his shield in his right hand, or if Nick Fury had a patch on his right eye instead of his left. . . . A casual reader might not notice these things during a quick read, but any comic book fan or creator would definitely notice the difference."[24] The bet paid off, as Tokyopop's authentic manga earned huge sales. The company also saved twenty to thirty dollars a page on translation and lettering fees. Many other companies entered the authentic-manga field, and by 2007 manga was the fastest-growing segment in American publishing.

Words in Context

cosplayers
Fans of manga and anime who dress up as their favorite characters, often at conventions.

Non-Japanese Manga

While purists insist that genuine manga is created only in Japan, manga-style comics are now produced worldwide. The Japanese government labels these productions international manga to differentiate them from homegrown material. They are also called global manga or original English-language manga. Some of the first non-Japanese manga came from Antarctic Press in the mid-1980s. Antarctic published *Mangazine*, an anthology of manga-style comics, and also the long-running *Ninja High School*. Their first titles featured black and white newsprint pages and wide-eyed, spiky-haired characters but were read from left to right like ordinary Western comics. Marvel Comics, which had flirted with the form in 1979's *Shogun Warrior*, created a Marvel Mangaverse series in 2000 with manga-style illustrations of Marvel characters. For example, the Mangaverse Iron Man looked much like Go Nagai's super robot Mazinger Z. Tokyopop has also promoted the art form with its Rising Stars of Manga contests, in which prospective manga artists submit stories in a variety of categories and the winners get the chance to create their own series.

While the Japanese regard manga as their own cultural creation, they are notably generous about praising manga artists in other countries. The first annual International Manga Awards in 2007 recognized Chinese artist Lee Chi Ching for his series *Sun Zi's Tactics*. Among the honorees at the 2014 ceremony were artists from Thailand, the United States, Spain, and Belgium.

In the late 1980s anime also began to break through to the wider US market. Again Otomo's *Akira* played an important part, this time in its anime version. American fans and critics alike recognized that this was not just another science-fiction saga for casual viewers but a dark epic with amazing imagery and multiple layers of meaning. Janet Maslin's review in the *New York Times* was typical:

> Mr. Otomo invests this dark flowering of post-nuclear civilization with a clean, mean beauty. The drawings of Neo-Tokyo by night are so intricately detailed that all the individual windows of huge skyscrapers appear distinct. And these night scenes glow with subtle, vibrant color. Never resorting to the gaudiness of much ordinary animation, Mr. Otomo uses a wide range of colors in thoughtful, interesting ways, and he enlivens his film with a constant sense of surprise.[25]

In the early 1990s anime viewing clubs formed in major US cities and on college campuses. The most dedicated clubs obtained videotapes from Japan of cutting-edge series. Some began to produce their own subtitled versions of these tapes using translated scripts. This practice, called *fansubbing*, was illegal but increasingly widespread. Small companies selling these fansubbed anime tapes enabled fans to obtain anime that was otherwise unavailable in the United States. *Neon Genesis Evangelion* was just one of the anime classics originally sold in fansubbed versions. At the same time, several domestic companies began to license and release Japan's anime hits for the growing American market. Today anime fan conventions, or cons, such as Sakura Con in Seattle and Anime Expo in Los Angeles, draw crowds from all over the United States. Anime has become a staple of TV networks, DVD rentals, and digital streaming services. Director Quentin Tarantino included an anime sequence in *Kill Bill: Vol. 1.*, and major Hollywood studios have announced production of live-action versions of anime such as *Akira* and the hyper-violent *Kite*. Once merely the province of American fans yearning for something different, anime and manga are now a significant part of American pop culture.

Words in Context

fansubbing
Anime fans' practice of illegally adding subtitles to imported anime.

The Future for Manga and Anime

Despite their status in the global culture and marketplace, manga and anime have both seen a downturn in sales and interest in the last few years. Young people in Japan and around the world are more interested in messaging and playing games on cell phones than reading manga or watching anime. The ease of downloading anime illegally has hurt revenues, as have the shrinking population and economic problems in Japan. Companies are experimenting with online distribution, but they have a hard time competing with all the free material available. As the market contracts, only a few major series in manga and anime are able to make lots of money. And Japanese artists in these genres generally work in modest surroundings, much like their great predecessor Osamu Tezuka. As blogger Dan Kanemitsu observes, "Just because you might think the stuff that comes from Japan is top-notch, it doesn't mean we secure top-notch compensation. Most US TV and

Neon Genesis Evangelion (pictured) was originally sold in a fansubbed version in the United States. Fansubbing began with devoted anime viewing clubs producing their own subtitled versions of anime series available only in Japan.

cable program producers would burst out laughing if they heard what kind of budgets we work under, so reducing our cost any further on the creative side would be very difficult."[26] Yet sharp, imaginative manga and anime titles continue to appear. As sales decline, sophisticated readers seem interested in more complex, arty productions again. Perhaps today's situation is just a lull before another boom occurs. Perhaps another Tezuka or Miyazaki is preparing a milestone manga or anime that will soon thrill fans all over the world.

Source Notes

Introduction: Anime and Manga

1. Quoted in Brooks Barnes, "Swan Song Too Hawkish for Some," *New York Times*, November 5, 2013. www.nytimes.com.

Chapter One: Manga: Pioneers and Early Development

2. Quoted in Matt Thorn, "A History of Manga," *Manga-gaku*, 2012. www.matt-thorn.com.
3. Helen McCarthy and Katsuhiro Otomo, *The Art of Osamu Tezuka: God of Manga*. Ilex, 2013. www.ilex-press.com.
4. Danny Choo, "Disposable Manga," Culture Japan. www.dannychoo.com.
5. Frederik L. Schodt, *Manga! Manga! The World of Japanese Comics*. New York: Kodansha, 2012, p. 63.

Chapter Two: Manga Becomes a Mature Art Form

6. Schodt, *Manga! Manga!*, p. 18.
7. Jacqueline Danziger-Russell, *Girls and Their Comics: Finding a Female Voice in Comic Book Narrative*. New York: Scarecrow, 2012, p. 140.
8. Masami Toku, "Shojo Manga! Girls' Comics! A Mirror of Girls' Dreams," in *Networks of Desire*, Minneapolis: University of Minnesota Press, 2007, p. 25.
9. Matt Thorn, "A History of Manga."
10. Schodt, *Manga! Manga!*, p. 23.

Chapter Three: The Early Years of Anime

11. TV Tropes, "Anime: Speed Racer." http://tvtropes.org.

12. Thomas LaMarre, *The Anime Machine: A Media Theory of Animation*. Minneapolis: University of Minnesota Press, 2009, pp. 17–18.

13. Jonathan Clements and Helen McCarthy, *The Anime Encyclopedia: Revised and Expanded Edition*. Berkeley, CA: Stonebridge, 2006, p. 716.

14. Gilles Poitras, *Anime Essentials: Every Thing a Fan Needs to Know*. Berkeley, CA: Stonebridge, 2001, pp. 18–19.

Chapter Four: Anime's Worldwide Success

15. mustang 87, *Hubpages* (blog), "Cartoon Network: Then and Now," May 17, 2012. http://mustang87.hubpages.com.

16. Clements and McCarthy, *The Anime Encyclopedia*, p. 612.

17. Poitras, *Anime Essentials*, p. 35.

18. Quoted in Toshio Suzuki, interview, included with *My Neighbor Totoro* DVD, Disney/Studio Ghibli, 2010.

19. Helen McCarthy, *Hayao Miyazaki: Master of Japanese Animation*. Berkeley, CA: Stonebridge, 2002, p. 10.

20. Quoted in Sean O'Connell, "From Wolf Gods to Moving Castles, a Beginner's Guide to the World of Hayao Miyazaki," ScreenCrush, September 5, 2013. http://screencrush.com.

Chapter Five: Anime and Manga:
Fans and Future Prospects

21. Michael Mammano, "The Sailor Moon Reboot: What We Know and What to Expect," Den of Geek, June 5, 2014. www.denofgeek.us.

22. Patricia Hernandez, "What *Pokémon* Is," *Kotaku*, October 11, 2013. http://kotaku.com.

23. Melia Robinson, "An Introduction into the Wild World of Cosplay," *Business Insider*, October 13, 2013. www.businessinsider.com.

24. Quoted in Jason Thompson, "Jason Thompson's House of 1000 Manga: A Quick and Dirty History of Manga in the US," *Anime News Network*, March 21, 2013. www.animenewsnetwork.com.

25. Janet Maslin, "A Tokyo of the Future in Vibrant Animation," *New York Times*, October 19, 1990. www.nytimes.com.
26. Dan Kanemitsu, "Analyzing the State of the Anime and Manga Industry in 2012," *Dan Kanemitsu's Paper Trail* (blog), March 19, 2012. http://dankanemitsu.wordpress.com.

For Further Research

Books

Jonathan Clements, *Anime: A History*. London: British Film Institute, 2013.

Jonathan Clements and Helen McCarthy, *The Anime Encyclopedia: Revised and Expanded Edition*. Berkeley, CA: Stonebridge, 2006.

Patrick W. Galbraith, *The Otaku Encyclopedia: An Insider's Guide to the Subculture of Cool Japan*. New York, NY: Kodansha USA, 2014.

Paul Gravett, *Manga: 60 Years of Japanese Comics*. London: Laurence King, 2008.

Helen McCarthy, *Hayao Miyazaki: Master of Japanese Animation*. Berkeley, CA: Stonebridge, 2002.

Frederik L. Schodt, *Manga! Manga! The World of Japanese Comics*. New York: Kodansha, 2012.

Websites

Anime.com (www.anime.com). This online magazine site features reviews of DVDs, manga, books, and toys, plus related news about Japanese culture and animation from other countries.

Anime News Network (www.animenewsnetwork.com). This site is the premier source of current news and information about anime, and it includes a helpful online encyclopedia and informed reviews and columns.

GhibliWiki (www.nausicaa.net). This wiki site is dedicated to collecting and presenting information about Studio Ghibli's films and animators, particularly Hayao Miyazaki.

Gilles' Service to Fans Page (www.koyagi.com). This personal site of author and anime expert Gilles Poitras is essential for fans seeking information not readily available elsewhere online.

JAI² (www.jai2.com). This is the personal site of Frederik L. Schodt, the foremost manga expert in the West and writer about Japanese history and culture.

Manga Here (www.mangahere.com). This site features news and updates about the latest manga releases in all categories.

Midnight Eye (www.midnighteye.com). This site is dedicated to providing articles, reviews, and interviews about Japanese cinema, including anime.

Otaku USA (www.otakuusamagazine.com). A site that provides a strictly American view of pop culture in Japan, including anime, manga, games, merchandise, and cosplay.

Tezuka in English (http://tezukainenglish.com). This site contains a great deal of information for English-speaking fans about all aspects of the great Osamu Tezuka's career and productions.

Index

Picture Credits